MISCARRIAGE
JUSTICE

THE MURDER OF TERSEA DE SIMONE

MURDER AND MAYHEM SERIES #6

FERGUS MASON

Absolute Crime Press
ANAHEIM, CALIFORNIA

Copyright © 2020 by Golgotha Press, Inc.

All rights reserved. No part of this publication may be reproduced, distributed or transmitted in any form or by any means, including photocopying, recording, or other electronic or mechanical methods, without the prior written permission of the publisher, except in the case of brief quotations embodied in critical reviews and certain other noncommercial uses permitted by copyright law.

Limited Liability / Disclaimer of Warranty. While best efforts have been used in preparing this book, the author and publishers make no representations or warranties of any kind and assume no liabilities of any kind with respect to accuracy or completeness of the content and specifically the author nor publisher shall be held liable or responsible to any person or entity with respect to any loss or incidental or consequential damages caused or alleged to have been caused, directly, or indirectly without limitations, by the information or programs contained herein. Furthermore, readers should be aware that the Internet sites listed in this work may have changed or disappeared. This work is sold with the understanding that the advice inside may not be suitable in every situation.

Trademarks. Where trademarks are used in this book this infers no endorsement or any affiliation with this book. Any trademarks (including, but not limiting to, screenshots) used in this book are solely used for editorial and educational purposes.

ABSOLUTE CRIME

www.AbsoluteCrime.com

Table of Contents

About Absolute Crime *8*

Introduction: The Strangler *11*

Explanation *17*

The Victim *24*

The Crime *29*

The Confession *44*

The Trial *60*

Confusion *69*

Inside *76*

DNA *82*

New Directions *94*

The Killer *100*

Aftermath *110*

Ready for More? *121*

Newsletter Offer *127*

ABOUT ABSOLUTE CRIME

Absolute Crime publishes only the best true crime literature. Our focus is on the crimes that you've probably never heard of, but you are fascinated to read more about. With each engaging and gripping story, we try to let readers relive moments in history that some people have tried to forget.

Remember, our books are not meant for the faint at heart. We don't hold back--if a crime is bloody, we let the words splatter across the page so you can experience the crime in the most horrifying way!

If you enjoy this book, please visit our homepage (www.AbsoluteCrime.com) to see other books we offer; if you have any feedback, we'd love to hear from you!

Sign up for our mailing list, and we'll send you out a free true crime book!

http://www.absolutecrime.com/newsletter

Introduction: The Strangler

Southampton, England – December 5, 1979

Teresa wasn't having a good night.

It had started off well enough. The 22-year-old clerk had spent most of the evening in her second job as a barmaid at the Tom Tackle, a popular bar in the center of Southampton. She'd taken on the bar job to make some new friends and keep up the payments on her used Ford Escort, and it had worked out well. She was cheerful and willing to work hard, and she'd quickly become a favorite of the regulars who drank there most nights and the after-theater crowds on the weekends.

That Tuesday the bar closed at 11:00pm, and normally Teresa would have had to remind customers of the 15 minute drinking-up-time rule, then wash the last glasses. Her friend Jenni was waiting for her at the bar, though, and bar manager Anthony Pocock knew the two girls were planning on going out. It was Jenni's birthday and rather than wait for the weekend they wanted to spend a couple of hours dancing. Pocock didn't mind washing a few glasses himself – he was happy to do a favor for his bubbly young barmaid. He'd let Teresa go as soon as the bar stopped serving, and the two of them had jumped in Jenni's car and headed off to a local disco. It would have been easy to walk – it wasn't far - but both girls felt safer driving. Southampton isn't known for abnormally high crime rates but it is a port city, and docks can attract rough people. Sometimes they wander into town in search of fun – or victims. So they drove to the club, and Teresa left her own car in the Tom Tackle's car park. After their night out Jenni could drop her off and she would drive home. It seemed a fair enough plan, and Teresa had no trouble with avoiding alcohol – she preferred to do so anyway when she was working the next day. What could go wrong?

This could go wrong. Now she was gasping for breath, the gold chain of her own crucifix looped tightly around her throat and starving her brain of oxygen. Hovering on the edge of blacking out, she was only dimly aware of her attacker ripping at her pantyhose and underwear with his free hand. Her skirt had already been pulled up and her blouse hung open. Her waning consciousness was still sluggishly trying to catch up. It was only minutes since she'd said goodnight to Jenni. The ruby glow of lights as her friend braked at the car park exit hadn't faded from her eyes before this hideous assault had begun. Too weak to struggle now, she could only wonder why it was happening as the strangler tried to force himself into her unwilling body.

Teresa wasn't having a good night, and it was going to be her last.

[1]

EXPLANATION

Kingston Cemetery, Portsmouth, England - August 12, 2009

The gravediggers hoped it wouldn't rain. It had held off so far but threatening clouds painted the sky an unseasonal gray. Rain was bad enough when you had to dig a new grave. Even if you set up a shelter over the hole water would seep down through the heavy clay soil and form a layer of thick, clinging sludge at the bottom. Sticky clots would weigh down the shovel's blade with every scoop, and clung to boots and clothing. It turned the job into a grinding, unpleasant struggle. It was a lot worse when it was an exhumation. Digging down towards a decayed casket and its contents was never a welcome task anyway. This grave had been closed for nearly 21 years and the most offensive stages of decomposition would be over, but clay is a wet soil and that can do unpleasant things to a corpse. Letting more water in as they dug wasn't going to improve it any.

Normally the gravediggers would have left the task for another day. That wasn't an option though. The grave they were opening was covered by a blue and white police tent. A reopened investigation needed a DNA sample from the cadaver beneath it, the remains of a 26-year-old felon who'd asphyxiated himself with a plastic bag in 1988. He'd spent much of his short life in prison for a long list of burglaries and armed robberies, but that wasn't what the police were interested in now. DNA traces from an old semen sample had given a partial match to the dead man's sister. Once the corpse was dug up a new sample would be taken, and that was expected to give a perfect match. If it did then he would be pinpointed as the man who'd raped and strangled Teresa de Simone in 1979, clearing up an old mystery that had seen an innocent man spend decades in jail for a crime he hadn't committed.

Five months before the shovels bit into Kingston Cemetery's damp clay, a mentally disturbed petty thief called Sean Hodgson had been released from prison after DNA tests showed he couldn't have raped and murdered Teresa. He had repeatedly confessed to the crime – one of seven men who'd done so – and police thought he'd known too much about the details of the murder for his confession to be a fantasy. By the time he'd realized the seriousness of the game he was playing and withdrew his confession it was too late – he was in court and the jury didn't believe him. He'd inflicted needless pain on the dead girl's parents, smeared the reputation of his own family and condemned himself to 27 years in prison out of a perverted desire to get attention. Now his innocence had been confirmed, however, and the newly rediscovered evidence that had done that also pointed to the real killer.

The grave was a simple one. There was no headstone, and the mound of dirt that had marked it when it was fresh had settled. The English don't embalm their dead, or use elaborate grave liners in a futile attempt to hold back decay – they simply let nature take its course and level the surface with fresh earth when it subsides. The grass over the plot was mown short, and it was bare of any decoration. Nobody had laid flowers here for a long time, which at least made things easy. The gravediggers set to work. They'd already laid sheets of plywood over the neighboring plot to avoid making a mess of it. Now they cut around the outline of the grave with their shovels, removed the turf in neat squares and placed it carefully face down on the grass. They'd need it later, when they closed the grave again. Finally a rectangle of heavy reddish soil confronted them. It was time to start digging.

One at each end of the cleared patch, they stamped their shovels into the ground and bent to their task. The first clods of clay thudded on the plywood. Standing along the cemetery paths to keep ghouls and photographers away from the section they'd closed off were officers from Hampshire Constabulary. They sweated slightly despite being in shirtsleeves, thanks to their anti-stab vests and traditional high helmets. The weather was humid and sticky, one of them thought as he glanced upwards, but those clouds looked nasty. He hoped it wouldn't rain.

[2]

THE VICTIM

It's hard to build up much of a picture of Teresa Elena de Simone from the available details. She was born in 1957, the only child of Mario and Mary de Simone. Her parents separated when she was young and Mary later remarried, this time to Michael Sedotti. Teresa kept her birth name. She was known as a shy girl who in her mother's words "wouldn't hurt a fly," but she did have some friends and after leaving school she managed to land a full-time job as a clerk with the Southern Gas Board, a state-owned energy giant that handled natural gas supplies to homes in the south of England and also ran a chain of stores selling gas stoves, furnaces and heaters.

In the fall of 1979 Teresa started looking for a part-time bar job. She had two motives for this. She wanted some extra income to help her with the payments on the car she'd recently bought, a used brown Ford Escort; she also thought it would be a good way to widen her social circle and make new friends. In late September she went for an interview at the Tom Tackle and Anthony Pocock, the manager (known as a landlord in Britain) who ran the bar for the Watney Mann brewery company, was impressed by her good nature. He thought she would fit in well at his bar, which had a steady crowd of regulars but also got a lot of after-show business from the theater, so he offered her two nights' employment every week. She quickly became popular with the other staff and customers, and after two months was a familiar and well-liked face among the clientele. That's not to say there wasn't gossip – rumors circulated that Pocock had begun an affair with her.[1] That seems unlikely though. The Sedottis were Roman Catholics and Teresa herself was at least moderately religious. The gold crucifix she was wearing the night she died was a regular feature among her jewelry.

Teresa was, before anything else, a sensible girl. She enjoyed nights out with her friends but would never do anything reckless like drive under the influence of alcohol. She'd also have known enough to steer clear of any risky situations when she was alone after dark. She had a kind heart, though; if she thought someone needed help she'd have offered it, even something as small as giving them the time. Unfortunately not everyone who asks for help is genuine. Teresa hadn't built up enough life experience to know that yet. She wasn't going to get the chance.

[3]

THE CRIME

The Tom Tackle – now renamed The Encore, to give it a more theatrical air - isn't a traditional English pub, with wooden beams and horse brasses beside an open fire. It takes up the ground floor of a 1960s concrete building on Southampton's busy Commercial Road. The bar itself has outside walls faced in red brick, making it a bit more attractive from the street, and it does its best to generate some character. It's a large bar and usually a crowded one. On weekends it pulls in a lot of business from the theater (named the Gaumont in 1979, now called the Mayflower) next door. These days it also attracts people looking for a meal, but English bar food in the late 1970s was usually restricted to potato chips, peanuts and maybe a few tired ham and cheese sandwiches in a plastic box beside the till. In 1979 people went to bars to drink and their thirst could keep the bar staff busy. Anthony Pocock was behind the bar himself most nights but used a string of part-time barmaids like Teresa to help out.

Until the licensing laws were relaxed by Tony Blair's government in 2003 the traditional closing time for British bars was 11:00pm. Landlords could apply for a late license for a special occasion, or a regular one for Friday and Saturday nights, but the majority of the time the last pints were poured at eleven. An almost ritualistic process was followed at the end of every night. British alcohol laws make it mandatory to call last orders quarter of an hour before closing time, often by ringing a bell, and that always prompts a last-minute rush. Once the bar has closed there's another quarter of an hour for drinking-up time, when customers can't buy any more drinks but can finish the ones they have. After the end of drinking-up time it's illegal to have alcohol in your hand. That last half hour is usually the busiest time of day for the bar staff, first making sure the final orders are all filled and nobody goes away disappointed, then – first gently, then insistently – chivvying everyone out the door.

Teresa was good at persuading people to drink up and leave; even a drunk who'd get belligerent to show he wasn't scared of the landlord was unlikely to cut up rough with a pretty young girl. She was always willing to do her share of the final cleanup too, once the customers had gone. On December 4, though, her friend Jenni Savage was patiently waiting at the bar. Pocock knew that today was Savage's birthday and she and Teresa planned to go out for a short celebration after her shift. Although it was a Tuesday night there were discos open, but none of them late – the last ones would close around 1:00am. Pocock knew that the 30 or 40 minutes it would take to wash the glasses, empty the ashtrays and clean the bar would take a big bite out of the girls' time, and he liked the young barmaid. When the second bell went to announce the till was closed he told her to get out of there – he'd clear up himself.

Behind the Tom Tackle was a small parking lot, where staff and those customers who ignored the government's ongoing DUI campaign would park their cars. Savage had left hers there when she'd arrived at the bar, and Teresa had parked hers when she came to work. The disco they wanted to go to wasn't all that far away – hardly more than half a mile on foot. The streets could get lively as the bars started to empty out, though, and both girls preferred safe to sorry. They got into Savage's car and minutes later were parked near the disco on London Road.

Teresa and Savage were both driving and they weren't about to ignore the daily TV commercials about the dangers of mixing alcohol and automobiles, so they stuck to soft drinks. They spent a couple of happy hours chatting and dancing anyway. Finally it was time to go – the club closed at one, and they both had to work the next day. Slipping out just before one to avoid the rush they returned to the car. Savage headed back down London Road, turned right onto Cumberland Place, followed its curve around then took another right onto Commercial Road. On their left was a low brick office building, then the Gaumont Theatre, and then the Tom Tackle. Savage turned off and drove round the back of the bar, pulling up next to Teresa's Escort.

It was late, but the streets were quiet and this was familiar ground for Teresa. She wished Savage a good night and got out of the car, then fumbled in her bag for her keys. As Savage pulled back onto Commercial Road a dark shape detached itself from the trees beside the car park, but Teresa didn't notice. She was busy getting the door open, slinging her coat and bag across to the passenger seat and climbing in. Finally she closed the door, locked it and reached for her seat belt.

As she was about to push her key into the ignition she heard a sudden rap on the glass beside her. Startled, she looked out. A young man – hardly more than a boy – stood there, pointing at his wrist in an unmistakable gesture. She would have simply shown him her watch through the window but it was too dark for him to see it. Anyway he looked so young; she didn't find him at all threatening. She rolled down the window to tell him the time.

As soon as the window opened wide enough the young man lunged at Teresa and seized her wrist. He reached down inside the car, unlocked the door and yanked it open. Then he forced himself into the driver's seat beside her, slammed the door loudly enough to alarm residents in Wyndham Court and grabbed her throat to muffle her outraged, frightened screams. As he twisted the collar of her blouse the heavy gold chain of the crucifix she wore tightened against her larynx, and she immediately began to gasp and choke as her airway was squeezed shut. The killer ignored her panicked attempts to breathe. He locked the car door to cut off her escape and began fumbling with her blouse, exposing one breast, then pulled her skirt up around her waist. He yanked violently at her pantyhose, ripping it down so brutally that one leg was torn from the other. Her panties were ripped away and thrown into the passenger footwell. Then, finding the driver's seat too cramped, he hauled his now almost unconscious victim out of her seat, somehow got her into the back of the two-door compact and raped her viciously. At some point in the process he finished strangling her to death.

When Teresa's mother woke up and found her daughter hadn't returned home she was immediately concerned. It wasn't like Teresa to stay out without letting her know, and she told her husband she was worried. Michael Sedotti drove to the Tom Tackle and saw Teresa's car in the parking lot, but he didn't enter the lot and check it closely. Instead he drove home to tell his wife what he'd seen.

Just before ten o'clock Anthony Pocock arrived back at the Tom Tackle. He was expecting a delivery from the brewery that morning2 and was annoyed to see Teresa's car still parked behind the bar. The delivery truck had to be able to pull up against the rear of the building so the heavy kegs could be lowered down the hatch into the beer cellar, and the brown Escort was blocking the space. There was no point calling Teresa and asking her to come by and move it; as far as Pocock knew she would be at her day job with the gas board. He decided to see if it was unlocked – if it was perhaps he could release the parking brake and roll it out of the way himself. Walking over to the little car he checked the driver's door. It was unlocked all right, but as he pulled it open he saw Teresa. She was sprawled across the back seat, naked from the waist down. Her right leg rested against the back of the seat and the left trailed into the footwell, exposing her bloodied genitals. One pale breast hung from her torn blouse, congealed froth trickled from her mouth and there was a band of abrasions around her throat. The stunned landlord realized instantly that she must have been murdered, and ran inside to call the police.

The first policemen to reach the parking lot concurred with Pocock – this was a homicide scene. A pathologist arrived at around 11:45am and carried out an initial examination of the corpse. He quickly confirmed that the victim had been subjected to an extremely brutal rape and had been strangled to death. It was no ordinary strangulation either. The froth around her mouth and the multiple lines of marks on her throat showed that her death had been a prolonged one. Using a ligature – as had happened here – it's possible to strangle someone into unconsciousness in ten seconds and kill them in a few minutes, but Teresa had been subjected to a much longer assault. When her body was taken to the morgue for a more in-depth examination the full horror became obvious. There were ten red marks round her throat, indicating that the asphyxiating pressure had been released then reapplied that many times. The rape had been violent enough that her vagina had been split, and other damage suggested she had been anally violated as well. Swabs were taken and revealed that her vagina was full of semen, enough of it that it must have got there shortly before her death. It also contained traces of blood. Type matching confirmed that this was a mix of her own Group B and the attacker's Group A or AB.

Homicide rates in Britain are low by global standards – the annual rate is 1.2 murders per 100,000 people, compared to 4.8 per 100,000 in the USA. It's a reasonably large country with a population of 60 million, however, so illegal killings aren't exactly unknown. Some of them get more attention than others, rightly or wrongly, and the brutal sex slaying of a popular, attractive young woman is likely to cause public outrage. At the time the attention of Britain's crime journalists was focused on the Midlands and north of England where a serial killer dubbed the Yorkshire Ripper had already killed eleven women, the most recent in early September. Teresa's death grabbed their attention and drew the media spotlight south for a few weeks. Initial inquiries drew a blank, of course, and the inevitable happened. Press interest slowly waned and drifted to other topics. The Ripper killed twice more in 1980. Police in north London wondered why so many young men and teenage boys were vanishing. Gradually these and other atrocities replaced Teresa's miserable death in the press and the public's imagination. The file remained open, though, constantly updated by Southampton police. The local CID detectives didn't forget Teresa and they quietly waited for a clue to her killer's identity. Then in late 1980 they got a phone call from a London prison officer. The clue they were looking for had surfaced.

[4]

The Confession

Sean Hodgson, his family and neighbors all agreed, was a normal teenager. "A nice quiet man," they say, "Kept to himself," even when all the evidence says otherwise. Born in Ireland in 1952, but brought up in County Durham after his family moved to northern England in the mid-1950s, Hodgson first fell out with the law as a preteen. He developed a taste for burglary and at eleven he was sent to one of the notorious "Borstal" special schools.3 These were designed to rehabilitate young offenders by detaining them in a reform school environment rather than an adult prison, but their reputation was mixed. The young inmates were kept away from hardened criminals successfully enough. The problem was that many of them were pretty hardened themselves, and the Borstals were tough and often violent institutions. There's no doubt that a spell in one was enough of a shock to many delinquents that they went straight rather than go back inside. That wasn't the case with Sean Hodgson.

In the decade and a half between Hodgson's release from Borstal and Teresa's murder he was arrested again and again. Burglary was a common charge. Theft from automobiles was another. Among these petty crimes were some hints of a darker pathology though. The UK has strict laws about going armed and Hodgson fell foul of them at least once, with a conviction for possession of an offensive weapon. Another conviction was for unlawful sexual intercourse, which means sex with a minor or someone else who can't give consent – in other words, rape. In 1978 he was diagnosed as having a severe personality disorder and being a compulsive liar. By this point he was a regular and heavy drug user, which likely didn't do his mental health any good.

Hodgson's whereabouts through much of the 1970s can be pinpointed quite accurately. That's because a lot of the time he was in a police cell or jail. He'd arrived in Southampton on the day of the murder, booked himself into a hostel and been arrested for theft within 48 hours. On December 7 he claimed to have knowledge about who had killed Teresa, and gave a statement to police that blamed an acquaintance of his for the murder. The police quickly checked out the man he'd named, but found that he had Group O blood and eliminated him as a suspect. Hodgson's own behavior was odd enough that he attracted some suspicion and the detectives tried to pin down his movements on that night, but couldn't find any details. All they had to go on was what Hodgson himself said, and they didn't believe him. There was no direct evidence linking him to the murder though, so his file went on the back burner. That would change a year later.

Meanwhile Hodgson just couldn't stay out of trouble. On May 16 1980 he was in Southampton Magistrate's Court pleading guilty to new charges of theft. He was bailed to await sentence, but before the sentencing hearing he was arrested yet again, this time in London, and charged with another list of offences. These centered around an illegal toolkit he'd been carrying, a toolkit designed to open automobile doors without a key. In mid-July a London court jailed him for three years and he was sent to Wandsworth Prison.

The Hodgson family were Irish Catholics, and Sean soon became a familiar visitor to the Catholic chaplain in Wandsworth. On December 11, 1980 he turned up in the prison chapel looking agitated. He wanted to take confession, he said; something was bothering him. Father Frank Moran had heard plenty of shocking confessions during his time at Wandsworth and he was about to hear another.

Moran listened as Hodgson explained that he was tormented by nightmares in which he saw the face of a woman he'd killed the year before. The anniversary of her death had just passed and he couldn't stand the guilt. Where had the murder taken place? Moran wanted to know. In Southampton. The confession was under the protection of the confessional booth, of course, but next day Hodgson spoke to an attorney then repeated it to a prison officer. The officer took notes of what he was hearing, as Hodgson described hitting the girl to keep her quiet, ripping her clothes and robbing her body. Next he wrote a note that gave the location of the murder as the Tom Tackle. By that time it didn't matter; everyone knew what killing he was talking about. Southampton Police were contacted and told that a Wandsworth inmate was confessing to the de Simone murder. Naturally they were interested. When they heard it was someone they'd already looked at for the killing they were even more interested. On December 15 a team from Southampton arrived at the London jail and started their interrogation of Hodgson.

Hodgson had already been caught several times in admitting to crimes he couldn't possibly have committed – including several that had happened while he was in a cell, and some more that had never happened at all – and if he'd stuck to a simple confession it probably wouldn't have been taken very seriously. He kept talking though, interview after interview, and the detectives quickly filled notebooks with details of the crime. Although the murder had generated a lot of media attention the police had kept several details quiet, a standard tactic to filter out crank confessions. The press had been told that Teresa had been strangled, but not how. Hodgson described a long, slow garroting and the foam that had bubbled from his victim's mouth. Newspapers had shown photos of a watch similar to the one stolen from Teresa's corpse, but the police had sat on the fact that someone had been trying to sell a matching one for cash around the city's bars; Hodgson told the officers how he had sold it to a man in a bar. He also told how the chain she'd been wearing around her neck had broken during the assault. Teresa's chain and crucifix had disappeared from her corpse. He described watching her get into the car; she'd sat on the seat with her legs outside, he said, then swung her legs in as she closed the door. The police asked Mary Sedotti to describe how her daughter had got into a car. It matched exactly. Hodgson told how he had left Teresa with her legs "in a funny position to describe," which certainly seemed to fit the crime scene.

Hodgson's account of the murder was eerily close to the facts, including almost all of the details the police had kept quiet. It was hard to believe that he got so many things right by simple coincidence. Had the detectives consciously or unwittingly coached him in what to say? There's no evidence to suggest that, although it's also impossible to rule out. Police interviews at that time weren't routinely taped, so the only records of the conversation were hand-written notebooks and the typed transcripts produced by the police themselves. Not all the paperwork from the case has survived. One thing that is known is that the interviewers asked Hodgson why he'd blamed another man for the murder. To take the heat off himself, he explained; wasn't that obvious?

The interviews were extensive. On December 19 Hodgson was brought to Southampton and the police asked him to show them his movements of that night. He did, and pointed out places where he said he'd disposed of some of Teresa's belongings. He made a sketch showing a distinctive section of wall and told the officers it was where he'd thrown her diary. The detectives found the photographs of where her handbag and purse had been recovered; the wall in the photos was a close match for the sketch. On December 21, back in Wandsworth, he asked to see a prison officer and launched into another detailed description of the crime, all delivered at breakneck speed. More damning nuggets went down on paper. Because he'd been drunk he had vomited as he walked away after the crime, he told the officer. The general area he described having puked in fit what a resident had reported immediately after the murder. Two days later Hodgson handed a policeman two notebooks and six sheets of paper in which he'd written yet another confession. This time he said he'd killed her because she had spurned his advances. It was a new element, and nobody really believed it, but it didn't contradict anything he'd said before.

Over the next weeks more written confessions were handed in by Hodgson or found in his cell. On Christmas Day he confessed to another murder, this time in London. The prison officer who read that confession told his superiors he thought it was "a load of shit."[4] This story didn't include the mass of detail his notes and statements about Teresa's death did. Neither did the next claim, on December 27, that he'd murdered a gay man in late 1978. The investigators had to look into the latest claims but they weren't very surprised to find out that neither murder had happened. In the meantime the details about Teresa kept coming. On January 2, 1981 Hodgson was interviewed again, and although his public defender advised him not to make a statement (and asked the police to note that fact) he told the detectives that he'd remembered more details. For the first time he said he'd raped Teresa – something he'd previously denied – and asked the cops if they'd recovered "the jacket which had slime from her vagina on it." He claimed to have violated her with a tire iron, which would have explained the internal injuries she'd suffered – yet another detail that hadn't been made public. He claimed that he'd left her with one leg up on the back parcel shelf and the other down behind the driver's seat. If she had been left in that position and the raised leg had fallen that could easily account for how she had actually been found, and that hadn't been revealed either. Then he described again how he had retched as he walked away from the scene. While he'd been doing that, he said, a light had come on in a nearby apartment and someone had looked out. The police knew that someone had indeed switched a light on and looked out.

On February 18 the police came back with some physical evidence. They asked Hodgson about a red pen marked with the logo of Ladbrokes, a popular chain of bookmakers.[1] He told them it was his and he'd last seen it the day of the murder. He had a matching green one, he said, which the police could find in among his belongings in the prison storage room. The detectives checked the sack of personal effects. There was a green Ladbrokes pen in there. Next was a black plastic comb that had been found on the floor of the car.

---

[1] Bookmakers are legal in the UK and there are branches of Ladbrokes in most towns.

Hodgson told them it was his, one he'd been issued during a previous spell in jail. He pointed out some scratches on it and said they were his initials. The cops sent the comb for forensic examination. The scratches had been made deliberately, the technician reported, and while it was hard to say if they were Hodgson's initials they certainly could be. Where was the comb from? Oh, said the technician, that was easy. It was a cheap type made on a Home Office contract for issue to prison inmates. Finally the police asked Hodgson about the set of skeleton keys that had been in his pocket when he was arrested in Trafalgar Square. He pointed one out and said it was a "jiggler," which could open and start any Ford car. He claimed to have used it to break into Teresa's car. The police tracked down an identical Escort and tried the jiggler on the locks. The doors opened.

Hodgson had confessed to killing Teresa and given a reason for the murder. He had confessed – both verbally and in voluntary written statements – many details of the crime, including several that had never been made public. There were skeptics among the investigators and they'd challenged him on several points, but each time he had come back with an answer that made sense if he was indeed the murderer. He had damned himself thoroughly out of his own mouth. Now there was just one more element required to link him firmly to the crime – his blood group. Because he had been looked at early in the investigation Southampton police already knew this. Hodgson's blood was Group A. That was enough. He was formally charged with the rape and murder of Teresa de Simone.

[5]

The Trial

In the British legal system serious crimes like rape and murder have to be tried by a judge and jury at a Crown Court. The Crown Court for Hampshire - the county where Teresa had been murdered - is in the county seat, Winchester. This ancient city was founded by the Romans on the site of an Iron Age market, and under Alfred the Great was the capital of the kingdom of Wessex. Later it became capital of the newly unified England, until London took over some time in the 12th century AD. Now it's a pleasant market town and the commercial and government center for a wealthy region of southern England. Sean Hodgson was brought there early in 1982 to face a jury for Teresa de Simone's rape and murder.

Hodgson had put a lot of effort into convincing people that he'd killed Teresa. First the investigating detectives, then the Director of Public Prosecutions[2] (a county government official responsible for deciding if a prosecution was in the public interest and if there was enough evidence to proceed) had looked at the case with initial skepticism but been persuaded by the mass of evidence contained in the repeated confessions. It's hard to under-

---

[2] At the time of the trial these decisions were made at the county level. Since 1986 a new national body, the Crown Prosecution Service, has handled the conduct of prosecutions for the whole UK.

stand why he did this. There's no question that he was mentally ill and had self-destructive tendencies. It's also obvious that he was an attention seeker. Does this fully explain his actions though? That's a difficult question. If he just wanted attention he was certainly getting it now. If he was trying to harm himself by earning a long term in jail, though, why did he do what he did next?

As the January 21 date for the trial approached, Hodgson started to back-pedal. He desperately assured his attorney that he was a fantasist who lied compulsively. The attorney was there to defend him and accepted that line as good enough to use in court. Hodgson had gone far beyond the point where a sudden claim of fantasizing was going to save him, though. His confession had turned the police spotlight on him and put him in the frame as a suspect, but the Crown weren't basing their case on it. If they had been then withdrawing it would have destroyed the case and let him walk free, but he'd added far too much detail and it had been too convincing. The prosecution case was built on a mass of circumstantial evidence, all of it thoughtfully verified by Hodgson himself, that put him at the scene of the crime when Teresa had died. It didn't matter if he retracted his admission of the rape and murder. He'd been seen leaving the scene and had admitted that was him. He had been arrested in possession of a device capable of opening the Escort's doors. His belongings had been found inside the victim's car and he'd confirmed they were his. He'd claimed to have been rejected by her, then she'd been found dead and splattered with semen that matched his blood group. He'd painted himself into a corner and there was no way out now.

When the trial opened the Crown's prosecutors laid out their case. Their account of Hodgson's actions that night largely matched his confessions, but to the dismay of the defense team the prosecution explained in painstaking detail how they had built up the sequence of events using only the other evidence. Every piece of it slotted neatly into place. The jury listened to the long litany of damning evidence. Presenting it and explaining its significance took most of the 15 day trial; the defense attorney's claims of fantasy were almost an afterthought, and the jury dismissed them contemptuously. Of course he was denying it now, they thought. He'd realized how serious it was now. This wasn't a stint in Borstal he was looking at, or a couple of years in jail for stealing automobiles. This was a Crown Court Judge who could put him away for life. His lawyer argued that he was a convincing liar. The jury agreed that he was convincing – he'd certainly convinced them – but they weren't buying the liar part.

Hodgson himself, stupid to the last, put the finishing touches to his own damnation. He refused to enter the witness box or submit to cross-examination. The jury never heard any alternative version of where he'd been that night and what he'd been doing. All they had to base their verdict on was a meticulous reconstruction bolstered by witness statements and physical evidence – none of which Hodgson was willing to argue with. They heard no reasons for the numerous confessions he'd voluntarily made. They heard no explanation for how he knew so much about Teresa's last moments and the condition of her body. Their decision was predictable. At 11:00am on February 5, 1982 they retired to consider the verdict. Barely three hours later they unanimously found Sean Hodgson guilty of the rape and murder by strangulation of Teresa de Simone. Judge Sheldon agreed. Since the abolition of the death penalty in 1967 there is only one possible sentence for murder in the UK, and that's life imprisonment. In Britain life is an open-ended term, but unless a "whole-life tariff" is set – that means the convict will die in jail – there's a minimum term to serve before they can apply for parole. For sexually aggravated murders like Teresa's the minimum term is 30 years. The British legal system is often criticized for being too lenient, and at lower levels it is, but things are different when you're staring down the barrel of a life sentence for murder. If the judge says 30 years then you're going to be behind bars 30 years from now. After that? Behave, show you've changed, and you might be lucky. Then again you might not. John Straffen died after 55 years in prison. Ian Brady was jailed in 1966 and isn't making any plans for his release.

One of the things you have to do to be eligible for parole is admit your guilt.

[6]

Confusion

The ink was barely dry on Judge Sheldon's signature when Hodgson's defense lawyer asked for permission to appeal the conviction. The application was based entirely on the validity of the confessions, and made several claims to explain why Hodgson's admissions had been so convincing:

1. Hodgson had picked up and assembled a considerable amount of information from TV and newspaper coverage of the murder.
2. He had put more details together from comments made by policemen during the interviews and the questions directed at him.
3. Intelligent guesswork had let him fill in many of the undisclosed details that police had relied on to screen out fake confessions.
4. By claiming ownership of objects found around the scene, and making observations about them, Hodgson had convinced police that these really were his possessions.

The application made sense; it was possible that Hodgson could have embellished his confessions using details obtained in these ways. Whether intelligent guesswork could have filled in all the gaps is up for debate of course. Lucky guesswork might be closer to the mark. The problem from the point of view of an appeal was to convince the review courts that this was a legitimate issue that hadn't been properly considered at the original trial. It was going to be difficult.

The appeal court looked at the application and compared it with the trial transcripts. Had Hodgson told the judge and jury that he'd been fantasizing and got in out of his depth? No, he hadn't. He had mentioned it in an unsworn statement but had refused to take the stand and give his version of events. As far as the appeal judges were concerned this wasn't a legitimate application; it was a new story that hadn't emerged before, and as far as they could tell its only purpose was to overturn a reasonable decision. In May 1983 Hodgson was denied leave to appeal;[5] if he wanted freedom he was going to have to wait until he was eligible to apply for parole in 2012.

Hodgson was starting a long jail term and in the eyes of the police and public the case was closed. It didn't completely fade away though. There had been several confessions before the trial, and late in 1983 there was another one. On September 17 a 21-year-old loner with a long criminal record told police that on the night of the murder he'd walked out of a care home in Portsmouth after stealing cash and a rucksack from a fellow resident, and made his way to Southampton. He had been loitering behind the Tom Tackle when Jenni Savage dropped Teresa by her car, and when Savage left he'd approached the vehicle and asked the time. Then when Teresa opened the window he'd grabbed her, forced his way into the car, raped her then strangled her with a seatbelt.

A jury had already sent someone to jail for Teresa's murder, but the police did their job anyway. They grilled the young man for details of the crime. As confessions went, they agreed, this one wasn't very impressive. The basics were close enough – hardly surprising after the publicity the investigation and trial had generated – but the rest of it was riddled with mistakes. He couldn't even describe the car accurately – he said it had four doors when it actually had two - or give details of the clothes he claimed to have ripped apart during the assault. This confession went in the crank file with the others; it did nothing to convince anyone that Sean Hodgson might not have been responsible. The young man was charged and jailed for the theft he'd just been picked up for, but he wasn't connected to the Tom Tackle murder. His confession wasn't taken seriously enough for Hodgson's legal team to be told about it. This has been criticized since – mostly by supporters of Hodgson - but it's hard to see what difference it could have made. A new application for appeal based on such a shoddy confession would have had no chance of success. There were now seven confessions to the murder and all bar one of them were completely unconvincing. The only one that looked genuine was Hodgson's.

[7]

Inside

Life in the British prison system is tough, but it's not quite as brutal as things can get in a US maximum security jail. How you get on depends on how you behave once you're inside the walls. You can do relatively easy time, or you can do hard time. Sean Hodgson seems to have set out to do the hardest time he could. Almost as soon as he was convicted he began fighting against the system, seemingly unaware of the fact that the system was infinitely more powerful than he was. To protest his innocence he launched into a series of hunger strikes and other minor rebellions. When he was jailed he'd had a girlfriend, a relationship that had somehow lasted for five years. Now he refused to let her visit him and told her to get on with her life,6 and the relationship quickly fell apart. Next he fell into a deep depression and ended up alternating between the hospital wing and suicide watch. By the mid-1980s his mental state had collapsed so badly that he was transferred to Broadmoor, a high security mental hospital that's used to hold some of the UK's most dangerously unbalanced murderers. Hodgson spent eight years there before being transferred back into the regular prison system. After his time in the hospital he spent the rest of his sentence in Her Majesty's Prison Albany.

HMP Albany is one of three high-security prisons on the Isle of Wight. The UK's equivalent of supermax prisons are the category A jails, where extremely dangerous killers and national security risks are incarcerated. As a category B prison Albany is one step down; nevertheless it's still a strictly controlled, virtually escape-proof joint packed with robbers, rapists and murderers. Albany exists to punish criminals and protect the public from them during their sentence, and most of the inmates are lifers, but at some point they'll be eligible for parole and they need to be ready to go back into society. That means the prison also has a full range of reintegration services to prepare them for that day. Therapy, education courses, vocational training and work experience are all available to inmates and they're strongly encouraged to take advantage. Hodgson refused.

He believed that joining any of the programs would be an admission of guilt.7 It's not really clear where he got that idea from, but he stuck to it for the entire time he was locked up.

Increasingly reclusive, Hodgson shut himself away in his cell for all but a few minutes every day. He refused to eat in the canteen with the other inmates; staff brought his meals to his cell. Almost the only times he left it was during the lockdown between 7:00pm and 7:00am; the computerized door system would allow each inmate out three times, for five minutes. The rest of the time he stayed in the locked 8 by 4 foot cell listening to the radio, reading courtroom dramas and writing letters to law firms. Most of the letters, he claimed, went unanswered. Perhaps that's true; on the other hand perhaps he didn't write as many letters as he claimed to have. He was hardly someone you could rely on to tell the truth, after all. It's not likely anyone would have been very interested in taking up his case anyway. The evidence of his guilt seemed overwhelming. Even from his cell, though, Hodgson could dimly sense that this might be changing.

[8]

DNA

When Hodgson was tried for Teresa's murder forensic science was far more limited than it is today. Samples of blood and other body fluids could be roughly matched by type, and this was a valuable tool for eliminating potential suspects – if someone had Group O blood there was no way they could have left Group A samples at a crime scene, for example. The science of genetics was steadily advancing, however, and it promised something better for investigators. In 1984 a team at Leicester University reported that they had developed a new technique based on DNA analysis.

DNA is the complex molecule that acts as instructions for a developing organism. It's not actually a blueprint, but as an analogy that's close enough for most purposes. What matters is that the DNA of any two humans is almost completely identical, because in both cases it contains all the information needed to grow a human, but it's not absolutely identical. The main function of DNA is to catalyze the production of proteins, but our genes contain a lot more DNA than is needed for that. Scientists call the excess "junk" DNA. Most of it isn't junk at all, of course; it has a whole range of other functions. Nevertheless, in among all this complex molecular machinery there are some oddities. Human DNA has been evolving for billions of years and it's collected some real junk in that time. Bits of viruses that infected a distant ancestor, obsolete code for fish features and many other fragments are hidden in among our mammal plans, and a lot of these fragments don't seem to do anything. Because of that random mutations can change them freely, without any adverse effects. The result is that 0.1% of our DNA can vary between individuals, and with billions of separate links in the chain there's almost no chance of two people having an absolutely identical sequence. In 1987 the Leicester University team formed a commercial testing laboratory and DNA profiling quickly became a feature of the justice system. If you have a DNA sample from the crime scene, and a suspect in custody, you could get a reliable yes/no answer very easily indeed.

It took a few years for anyone connected with Hodgson's case to see the implications of the new technology, but it seems that by 1998 someone was wondering if DNA profiling could clear his name. DNA tests for British criminal cases were carried out by the Forensic Science Service at the time, and that year a lawyer acting for Hodgson sent them a request for disclosure of evidence.8 What he was after was details of any semen samples that had been retained. Hodgson was in jail and willing to provide a DNA sample; if that could be compared with a sample from Teresa's body then, if Hodgson was innocent as he claimed, the comparison would prove it.

At this point history interfered. The Forensic Science Service had been set up as a government agency in 1991, and had taken over most forensic tasks from a collection of earlier, local and regional organizations. Methods (and standards) of record keeping among those older organizations hadn't been very consistent, so while the FSS had a large archive of exhibits and samples from pre-1991 cases it didn't have a completely reliable catalog of them. When Hodgson's lawyer asked if any samples were available the FSS couldn't find records of any, and replied that none had been retained. Hodgson was ill in the prison's medical wing at the time and couldn't give his lawyer any more instructions, so the inquiry fizzled out. It was nearly ten years before he picked up that trail again, this time with a new legal team.

The inside of a British jail isn't somewhere most people are eager to see, but once you end up in one there are a few amenities available. Free access to correspondence courses through the Open University, for example, or vocational training. There are several volunteer groups that work to rehabilitate and assist inmates. There's even a national newspaper just for those who find themselves on the wrong side of the bars. It's called Inside Time and it's a surprisingly interesting read. In its pages you regularly find letters and articles by prisoners complaining about changes to the rules, pointing out poor services or suggesting new ways to integrate ex-cons back into society. Prison officers have been known to reply, sometimes mercilessly demolishing the more way-out complaints ("Mr Starbuck complains about having to serve 11,000 days in custody and asks 'what's the point?' This is a good case of 'woe is me'")[9] and sometimes showing surprisingly sympathetic agreement with the prisoners' concerns. The paper also publishes Inside Information, a thick handbook packed with information on the corrections system that's supplied free to all prison libraries, and edits a book of poetry written by inmates. Of course all this publishing has to be paid for, and if you're looking for a reliable source of income advertising is rarely going to let you down. Given the intended readership of Inside Time it's no surprise that a lot of the ad space is bought by lawyers.

There are plenty of legitimate reasons why an inmate would want to talk to a lawyer. Preparing an appeal, getting ready for a parole application or fighting a new charge all mean legal advice is needed, and of course being in jail doesn't stop normal issues from rearing their heads. It can even make that more likely – cons have a high divorce rate, and divorce creates work for lawyers too. All this makes Inside Time a natural place for attorneys to advertise, whether they're a reputable firm or a shady ambulance chaser. In March 2008 Hodgson, leafing through his copy of Inside Time, found an advert for law firm Julian Young & Co. The firm specialized in appeals against conviction, and Hodgson thought that maybe they could have another shot at tracking down a sample from the original investigation. Julian Young were willing to give it a go and assigned lawyer Rag Chand to the case.

At first Chand had no more luck than the previous attempt. The FSS still couldn't find any remaining exhibits – or even paperwork – from the Tom Tackle case. Chand persevered. He spent four months searching through archives and using newspaper cuttings to build up a picture of what he was looking for and where it might be. Finally, in July 2008, he got lucky. He was able to point the FSS to a cache of evidence and documents stored in an industrial park in the Midlands, hundreds of miles to the north of the murder scene. The collection of exhibits and case files had been transferred to the FSS when it was formed but had never been itemized for their records; that was why earlier searches hadn't found it. Now they knew it existed, though, and the FSS rapidly sorted through it for anything related to Teresa's death. They found exactly what Chand had been looking for – the swabs taken from her body.10

With the swabs now located the Crown Prosecution Service requested a DNA sample from Hodgson and ordered a comparison to be carried out. The selected swabs were those from Teresa's anus and vagina; both of them contained DNA from her assailant. Julian Young were sent the initial results in December and on January 30, 2009 the CPS publicly announced their conclusion: the semen found in Teresa's body could not have come from Sean Hodgson. That opened the way for an appeal to be granted, and the CPS informed the Criminal Cases Review Commission that the Crown did not plan to fight the appeal. The case was scheduled for the Court of Appeal on March 18, 2009.

The case for the appeal was straightforward. It didn't attempt to lay any blame on the police who had investigated the crime or the court that had sentenced Hodgson. If it blamed anyone it was Hodgson himself; the appeal explained in detail how he had made multiple convincing confessions, appeared to have knowledge that could only have been possessed by the killer, and destroyed his own credibility in court by refusing to enter the witness box or submit to questioning. The grounds for appeal were simple and uncontroversial; new evidence, not available in 1982, had been discovered and it showed he simply couldn't have raped Teresa. With the appeal not being contested the result was a foregone conclusion. It was being heard by the Lord Chief Justice, the senior judge in the English legal system. The Chief Justice, the appropriately named Lord Judge, ruled that the conviction was unsafe and overturned it. There would be no new trial, because the evidence no longer justified investigating Hodgson's guilt; he was to be freed immediately.

But if Hodgson hadn't killed Teresa, who had?

[9]

NEW DIRECTIONS

The Forensic Science Service might not have had a perfect record when it came to organizing the evidence in its archives, but it was leading the way in other areas. The UK was the first nation to make widespread use of DNA profiling and the FSS quickly saw its potential. Starting from the early 1990s police forces began collecting DNA samples as a routine part of investigations, and the law allowed these to be retained if the suspect was later convicted of a crime (and, in many cases, even if they're cleared.) The FSS realized that as a high percentage of crimes are committed by recidivist criminals who have been convicted before, a library of samples would be a valuable tool. In 1995 they activated the world's first DNA database and it began growing rapidly. From now on a sample found at a crime scene could be quickly checked against the database.

Hodgson's release put the murder of Teresa de Simone back in the unsolved pile, but now there was a DNA sample to check and an extensive database to check it against. A new investigation, labeled Operation Iceberg, was launched to exploit the new evidence. The genetic profile of the rapist was fed into the search engine to see if he had been convicted of another crime since 1987, when the first samples had been collected. He hadn't; the search didn't find any record with the same genetic code as the sample from Teresa's corpse. However that didn't mean it was a waste of time.

A DNA match strong enough to identify someone as the source of a sample needs to show identical values across a number of points in the DNA string. In the UK tests use the SGM Plus matching system, which compares eleven points on the genome – one to confirm the gender of the subject, and ten to give a Yes/No match. If all eleven points match there's almost no chance of a false positive – the odds against it are more than the number of people alive today and approaching the total number who've ever lived. The search on the sample from Teresa didn't give that level of matching. It did find something though. Every baby that's born gets half their DNA from the mother and half from the father; the two sets of parental genes are randomly shuffled at conception. Random mutations add a few unique code segments in every generation. Because the genes inherited from each parent include a few of these, it's possible to tell that two samples came from people who are related. The search found a partial match – the DNA database contained a sample that probably came from a brother of Teresa's killer. The FSS technicians ran the sample again and got the same partial match. They pulled the name of the record from the database and tracked down their siblings. A brother was dead, a sister alive; a DNA sample was requested from the sister and yet another comparison was run. The same partial match came up. That pointed the finger squarely at the dead brother. His name was David Lace, and on September 17, 1983 – 18 months after Hodgson was convicted and jailed - he'd confessed to Teresa's murder.

[10]

The Killer

David Andrew Williams was born on September 2, 1962 in Portsmouth. His childhood was a troubled one, plagued by personality issues; by a young age he was seen as an aggressive, potentially violent loner. He quickly drifted away from his family and into trouble, and was constantly in and out of care homes and hostels. His biological family couldn't stand the strain and gave him up for adoption, after which he changed his name to David Lace to match his adoptive parents. He didn't fit in any better with them than with his real family, however, and his behavior drifted steadily into criminality. His first conviction came when he was just 15 years old; in November 1977 he robbed a house and was caught. Because of his age he evaded jail, but the experience didn't teach him anything positive. In August the next year he snatched a handbag from a woman in Portsmouth and was arrested again. This time he was ordered to live in a supervised hostel until he reached the age of 18. The problem with orders like this is they depend on the convicted lawbreaker obeying them and the likelihood of that can be guessed from the fact they broke the law in the first place. On December 4, 1979, three months past his 17th birthday,

David Lace ransacked the other rooms in the Portsmouth care hostel and stole a rucksack and all the cash he could find. Then he walked out the door and struck out towards Southampton. He arrived there late in the evening – it's a long walk, nearly 20 miles – and loitered around the downtown area. As he'd described in his 1983 confession, he had been behind the Tom Tackle when Jenni Savage dropped Teresa by her car. The rest had happened much as he described, even if he'd got many details wrong.

It's not hard to understand why the police discounted the confession. By the time Lace made it Hodgson had been convicted on the basis of what looked like solid evidence. Lace was the seventh person to confess and his account was far from the most accurate one. As well as getting significant details about Teresa's car and clothing wrong he made it clear that he wanted to be locked up.11 It was already clear that Lace didn't function very well outside an institution, and saying straight out that he wanted to be returned to one didn't help his credibility.

Routine inquiries were made as police followed up the confession – that was required even if they didn't take it seriously – but Lace wasn't in the frame at this point. It didn't make a lot of difference anyway – like Hodgson he was an incorrigible but useless criminal, and most of his time was spent in jail. In January 1980 he was convicted for the thefts from the Portsmouth hostel. In September of the same year he went inside for nine months after being convicted of a series of break-ins in Portsmouth. June 1984 saw him found guilty of robbing a post office at knifepoint; this time he got more serious time, a five-year sentence in HMP Dartmoor in Devon. He served three years of that and was released again in June of 1987. Before he'd always returned to his native Hampshire, but not this time. Perhaps he hoped a new location would help him turn his life around, or maybe he just liked the area he'd spent the last three years in. Dartmoor prison is a grim and antiquated edifice, surrounded by high grey granite walls, that was built in the early 19th century to hold French and American POWs. By the 1980s it was a Category C prison, the lowest category of "closed" jail. Inmates in Category C can't be trusted in an open prison but aren't thought likely to escape. If they behave and they're getting near the end of their sentence there are some opportunities for Dartmoor prisoners to leave the jail for work experience, and maybe

Lace decided he liked the area. Whatever was behind his decision, when he was released in 1987 he found himself a room in the nearby fishing port of Brixham and soon got a job on a trawler.

It seems like Lace really did feel remorse for what he'd done. He lived in Brixham for over a year without contacting his family. Then in fall 1988 he travelled back to Portsmouth for a visit. While he was there he told people that he was tormented by things he'd done, including a death he'd caused when he was young after things "got out of hand." Family members he visited got the impression he was trying to say goodbye.12 Coworkers in Brixham thought the same when Lace started giving away his belongings and talking about the remorse he felt for his previous actions. He quit his job and, increasingly depressed, withdrew into himself.

Friends last saw him on December 7 or 8, 1988. On December 9 his landlord knocked on the door of his room. There was no reply. When he broke open the door he found Lace sprawled lifeless on his bed. There were superficial slashes on his arms, a plastic bag over his head and he'd swallowed a handful of sleeping tablets. The death was ruled – to nobody's surprise – as a suicide and Lace was buried in Portsmouth. His grave was a simple one and got little attention from visitors.

With the DNA evidence now pointing to Lace as Teresa's killer the Operation Iceberg team wanted confirmation. That meant getting a sample of Lace's own DNA to confirm what had been suggested by his siblings' samples. It's not usually difficult to get an exhumation order in the UK if it's in connection with a murder inquiry, and this case was no exception. On

August 12, 2009 Lace's grave was opened and his body taken to a Portsmouth hospital's pathology department. There, police forensic technicians extracted several samples from the remains and started the complex chain of procedures needed to replicate the DNA code and compare it with the 1979 sample. On September 17 they announced the results of the test. It was a perfect match.

The leader of the Operation Iceberg team, Detective Chief Inspector Phil McTavish, announced that the DNA match was "overwhelming" evidence of Lace's involvement in Teresa's death and said that police were not looking for anyone else in connection with the case. Both McTavish and the CPS were careful to stress that without a trial and conviction nobody was saying Lace was guilty, but their meaning was clear – nearly 30 years after Teresa died her murder had been solved. Her mother and stepfather spoke publicly to express gratitude for the rapid pace of the new investigation and the quick identification of the killer, but also talked of their frustration that they would never know why Lace had committed the murder.[13]

Aftermath

Sean Hodgson was released from prison on March 18, 2009. In the UK prison system there's resettlement support available for inmates being released after serving their sentence, designed to reintegrate them into society and reduce the chance of them reoffending. That's not available to those released for other reasons though, so Hodgson wasn't eligible for it. He was given a one-off cash payment of £46 (about $70) and that was it as far as the prison system was concerned.

It wasn't all the money he had coming to him, however. Because he'd been imprisoned for a crime he hadn't committed – no matter that his imprisonment had been nobody's fault but his own – he was now entitled to compensation from the British government. The length of his incarceration meant the total he could get might be more than £1 million, in excess of $1.5 million. Because there was a possibility of him suing the Forensic Science Service, which might have brought in another large sum, it was obvious that it could take years to decide the final payment. Two MPs agitated to "cut through the red tape" to make an immediate payment, and a fund was set up with a starting value of £250,000 ($390,000.) Hodgson used the money to buy himself a house in the north

Yorkshire town of Bishop Auckland, near where he'd been brought up as a child. He gave interviews to the press about his new life and how he was overcoming the way he felt he'd been treated. His lawyer Julian Young told the local paper that Hodgson was "doing really well."[14]

Not everyone agreed. In August 2010 a 22-year-old woman with learning difficulties, a resident at a care home near Hodgson's new residence, complained that Hodgson had raped her. He was quickly arrested and charged. He denied raping his victim but admitted "sexual touching," probably on advice from Julian Young. Because of the victim's mental condition the prosecutor withdrew the rape charge but pressed for a conviction for sexual assault. At the May 2011 trial Young tried to blame the offence on his client's long imprisonment, but Judge Christopher Prince wasn't falling for it.

He left no doubt that he didn't care what grievances anyone had against the criminal justice system; his main concern, he said, was "to protect the public as much as is possible against any future offending by Hodgson."[15]

Hodgson evaded another jail sentence on the sexual assault charge but was given a three-year community order.[16] A community order is a punishment and rehabilitation program that can contain a number of elements. Common ones include regular meetings with a probation officer, a ban on entering designated buildings or areas, prohibitions on drinking alcohol or unpaid work in the community. Anyone who violates the terms risks being sent to serve out the rest of the term in jail. Hodgson was ordered to attend regular meetings with an offender management officer and get help for his alleged mental problems.

In August 2011 Hodgson was arrested again, this time for a DUI incident where he crashed his automobile into a bus. As well as being drunk he had been driving without insurance. In November he was stopped by the police, breathalyzed and arrested again for DUI and driving without insurance. The same month he was also reported for breaching his community order; another report followed in December, but by the time anyone acted on it Hodgson was already serving a ten-week jail sentence for the driving offences. While he was in prison he made it clear that he wasn't going to follow the terms of his community order when he was released. That was the wrong thing to say, because when the ten weeks was up nobody came to unlock the door. At a new court hearing on February 10, 2012 Judge Prince announced that Hodgson was refusing to comply with his community order, refused to change his drinking and drug habits – he'd been injecting heroin[17] - and was a danger to the public. The judge ordered a new psychiatric evaluation and told Young that Hodgson would stay in jail for at least another four weeks.

By this time Hodgson, now a wild-looking and unkempt figure with a scruffy mane of dirty white hair, was on a downward spiral of illness. His self-destructive lifestyle since leaving prison had taken a heavy toll on his already failing health and by summer 2012 he'd been released on medical grounds. His condition continued to worsen through fall. On October 28, 2012 he died of emphysema. He was 61 years old; nearly half his life had been spent in prison, mostly for a crime he hadn't committed.

Was Sean Hodgson a victim of injustice, as he was so often described by the British media? That depends on your point of view. He certainly spent 27 years in jail for something he didn't do. He wasn't an innocent victim caught in the jaws of a corrupt or incompetent legal system, though. Far from it. He repeatedly confessed to Teresa's murder and, when the police appeared skeptical or tried to demolish his confessions, gave them elaborate and convincing responses calculated to remove any doubts. It's hard to feel much sympathy for him. Clearly he was mentally ill even before he was convicted and jailed; his behavior makes that obvious. Britain has a National Health Service, though. Whatever its faults, and there are many, the system provides health care that's free at the point of treatment. Nobody is ever turned away because they can't pay, and if Hodgson needed treatment all he had to do was ask for it. The best way to ask is to go to a doctor and say, "I'm mentally ill and I need help." Going to the police and saying "I murdered a girl" isn't going to work.

Illness or not, Hodgson confessed to Teresa's murder because he wanted to be the center of attention. His grandstanding diverted attention from inquiries that could have led to the real killer, wasted countless hours of police time and landed the taxpayer with a huge bill for keeping him incarcerated. It played with the emotions of Teresa's family who first felt relief that the murderer had been caught, then were forced to watch as Hodgson wasted huge sums of public money on appeals and finally walked free. If he hadn't grabbed center stage it's possible Lace's 1983 confession would have been taken more seriously and his guilt could have been established while he was still alive. A trial and conviction might have given Mary and

Michael Sedotti the answers they were desperate for; instead all they got was a cursory apology from Hodgson as he walked out of prison. Within days he had returned to the antisocial lifestyle of drugs, alcohol and petty crime he'd been in so much trouble for before, this time paid for by taxpayers' money – not enough taxpayer's money apparently; he staggered, drunk, between central London's expensive bars while whining that he couldn't afford to eat.[18]

For anyone who's studied the case it's also hard to shake the suspicion that his knowledge of it came from more than a ghoulish interest in crime reporting and some lucky guesswork. The DNA evidence totally cleared him of raping Teresa, and Lace's confession to the actual murder seems to close the matter. Just how did Hodgson know so much about the state of the body, however? Did he stumble across the crime scene while prowling the streets looking for someone to steal from? Was his story of defiling her corpse with a tire iron true? Did he rob the dead woman of her watch and jewelry? The answers to those questions died with Sean Hodgson but there's no doubt that he was capable of theft and sexual assault.

Much of the press coverage has painted Hodgson as a victim, but if he was really a victim of anything it was his own stupidity. The true victim in all this was Teresa De Simone, and while Hodgson didn't kill her his actions helped shield the man who did. David Lace ended her life; Sean Hodgson tormented her in death. The only happy ending to this tragic tale is that the world is now rid of them both.

READY FOR MORE?

We hope you enjoyed reading this series. If you are ready to read similar stories, check out other books in the *Murder and Mayhem* series:

America's First Serial Killers: A Biography of the Harpe Brothers (By Wallace Edwards)
They murdered. They stole. And they did it all to excess. Unlike other bandits of early America, they didn't do it for the money--they did it for the thrill and love of blood. They were the Harpe Brothers, and they have been called America's first true serial killers.

In this gripping narrative, the crimes and the lives of America's most notorious sibling killers are documented like a page-turning novel.

Deadly Darlings: The Horrifying True Accounts of Children Turned Into Murderers (By William Webb)

If you've ever thought your child was bad, then you haven't seen anything yet! In the pages that follow, you are about to meet some of the most vicious children who ever lived.

The kids in this book are as young as ten-years-old and they are ruthless. The nice ones killed in cold blood—but many of these kids weren't nice…they wanted their victims to suffer.

Some were turned killers by their brutal home environments; others were just inherently evil. They were all deadly darlings you'd never want to meet on the street.

The Teacup Poisoner: A Biography of Serial Killer Graham Young (By Fergus Mason)
Graham Young had an unusual obsession from a young age. Where most youths might be interested in music and sports, Young was fascinated by poisons. By the age of 14, he was using his family (who, of course, didn't know) as experiments. In 1962, still a teen, his stepmother died from one of his poisoning experiments.

Young eventually confessed to the murder of his stepmother and the attempted murder of several other members of his family; he was sent to a mental hospital for nine years, where he was ultimately released fully recovered. Unknown to the hospital, however, Young was actually using his time in the mental hospital to study medical texts and improve his poisoning skills. His true work as a poisoner had only just begun!

This gripping narrative gives you a page-turning look at one of England's most notorious serial killers: Graham Young.

The Butcher Baker: The Search for Alaskan Serial Killer Robert Hansen (By Reagan Martin)
Beautiful Alaska--a peaceful, natural land where you know your neighbors and don't have to lock your doors. For most people, it's the perfect place to experience nature; for Robert Hansen, it was the perfect place for murder.

Between 1980 and 1983, Hansen went on a murderous rampage killing between 17 and 37 women in the Anchorage, Alaska area. Hansen, a small-business owner, and pillar of the community was also an avid hunter and used young girls as prey when he decided he needed a more challenging hunt.

This book is the gripping account of the hunt and eventual capture of an unlikely killer, who almost got away with it.

Mary Cecilia Rogers and the Real Life Inspiration of Edgar Allan Poe's Marie Roget (By Wallace Edwards)
The murder of Mary Rogers may not be well known today, but in the 19th century, it was one of the most compelling murders of the century. It became a national sensation--so much so that Edgar Allan Poe used it as the inspiration for his story "The Mystery of Marie Roget."

This chilling narrative will take you back in time to 1838, where you will learn the details of the case and how it became a national phenomenon.

No Guns Allowed On Casual Friday: 15 Of the Scariest Co-Workers You Will Never Want to Work With (By William Webb)
Almost everyone thinks it: "One day I'm going to give my boss what he has coming." The fifteen people in this book took this notion to the extreme.

What kind of workplace drives a person into performing such heinous acts? Does a workplace drive a person to kill, or is the killer already inside, waiting for a reason to act out? Find out in this fascinating quick read.

If you are stressed at work, then maybe this book will show you that you don't have it so bad; or maybe it will show you that the person in the cubicle next to you may need to be handled a little more…delicately.

NEWSLETTER OFFER

Don't forget to sign up for your newsletter to grab your free book:

http://www.absolutecrime.com/newsletter

Notes

[1] The Daily Mail, March 21, 2009, *I didn't kill her! 30 years on, former pub landlord named in barmaid murder case pleads his innocence*

[2] England and Wales Court of Appeal, *Regina V Robert Graham Hodgson*, Para. 9

http://www.bailii.org/ew/cases/EWCA/Crim/2009/490.html

[3] The Daily Telegraph, March 17, 2009, *Victim of Britain's 'longest miscarriage of justice' apologises for false confession*
http://www.telegraph.co.uk/news/uknews/law-and-order/5005718/Victim-of-Britains-longest-miscarriage-of-justice-apologises-for-false-confession.html

[4] England and Wales Court of Appeal, *Regina V Robert Graham Hodgson*, Para. 28

http://www.bailii.org/ew/cases/EWCA/Crim/2009/490.html

[5] England and Wales Court of Appeal, *Regina V Robert Graham Hodgson*, Para. 40

http://www.bailii.org/ew/cases/EWCA/Crim/2009/490.html

[6] The Guardian, April 28, 2009, *Freedom? It's lonely*
http://www.theguardian.com/society/2009/apr/29/sean-hodgson-release-prison

[7] The Guardian, April 28, 2009, *Freedom? It's lonely*
http://www.theguardian.com/society/2009/apr/29/sean-hodgson-release-prison

[8] England and Wales Court of Appeal, *Regina V Robert Graham Hodgson*, Para. 41

http://www.bailii.org/ew/cases/EWCA/Crim/2009/490.html

[9] Inside Time, Sep 2013, *A word from the other side*

http://www.insidetime.org/articleview.asp?a=1560&c=a_word_from_the_other_side

[10] The Guardian, Mar 18, 2009, *Miscarriage of justice victim served extra 11 years due to 'lost' evidence*

http://www.theguardian.com/uk/2009/mar/19/miscarriage-justice-hodgson

[11] Southern Daily Echo, Sep 17, 2009, *David Lace's confession*

http://www.dailyecho.co.uk/video/video/90086/

[12] Southern Daily Echo, Sep 17, 2009, *David Lace's life was a turbulent one, say police*
http://www.dailyecho.co.uk/news/briefing/teresa_de_simone/4634621.Background_to_the_life_of_Teresa_s_killer/

[13] Southern Daily Echo, Aug 12, 2009, *Teresa De Simone's parents will never know why she was murdered*
http://www.dailyecho.co.uk/news/4542055.Teresa_De_Simone_s_parents_will_never_know_why_she_was_murdered/?ref=rl

[14] The Northern Echo, Dec 10, 2009, *Sean building a new life*

http://www.thenorthernecho.co.uk/archive/2009/12/10/4787710.Sean_building_a_new_life/

[15] BBC News, May 13, 2011, *Miscarriage of justice victim sentenced for sex assault*
http://www.bbc.co.uk/news/uk-england-13391943

[16] The Northern Echo, Feb 11, 2012, *Injustice victim Sean Hodgson is still in jail*

http://www.thenorthernecho.co.uk/news/9525885.Injustice_victim_Sean_Hodgson_is_still_in_jail/

[17] The Guardian, Sep 18, 2009, *Sean Hodgson's fight for justice is still going on*

http://www.theguardian.com/theguardian/2009/sep/19/sean-hodgson-miscarriage-justice

[18] The Guardian, April 28, 2009, *Freedom? It's lonely*
http://www.theguardian.com/society/2009/apr/29/sean-hodgson-release-prison